Can Science Solve?

# The Mystery of Vampires and Werewolves

Chris Oxlade

Heinemann
LIBRARY

**www.heinemann.co.uk/library**
Visit our website to find out more information about **Heinemann Library** books.

To order:
☎ Phone 44 (0) 1865 888066
▤ Send a fax to 44 (0) 1865 314091
▣ Visit the Heinemann Bookshop at www.heinemann.co.uk/library to browse our
  catalogue and order online.

First published in Great Britain by Heinemann Library,
Halley Court, Jordan Hill, Oxford OX2 8EJ,
a division of Reed Educational and Professional Publishing Ltd.
Heinemann is a registered trademark of Reed Educational & Professional Publishing
Limited.

OXFORD MELBOURNE AUCKLAND
JOHANNESBURG BLANTYRE GABORONE
IBADAN PORTSMOUTH NH (USA) CHICAGO

Designed by AMR
Illustrations by Art Construction
Origination by Ambassador Litho Ltd
Printed in Hong Kong/China

ISBN 0 431 01622 4
06 05 04 03 02
10 9 8 7 6 5 4 3 2 1

**British Library Cataloguing in Publication Data**

Oxlade, Chris
  Can science solve the mystery of vampires and werewolves?
  1.Vampires – Juvenile literature 2.Werewolves – Juvenile
  literature
  I.Title II.Wallace, Holly, 1961– III.Vampires and
  werewolves
  398.2'1

**Acknowledgements**
The Publishers would like to thank the following for permission to reproduce
photographs: BBC Natural History: pp20-21; Corbis/Bettman: p4; DK Photos: p22; Dracula
Society: p28; Fortean Picture Library: pp7, 10, 12, 13, 15, 19, 26; Kobal Collection: p27;
Mary Evans Picture Library: p9; Oxford Scientific Films/Richard Packwood: p29; Robert
Harding Picture Library: p11; Science Photo Library: pp17, 18, 23, 25.

Cover photographs reproduced with permission of Moviestore Collection.

Every effort has been made to contact copyright holders of any material reproduced in
this book. Any omissions will be rectified in subsequent printings if notice is given to
the Publisher.

Any words appearing in the text in bold, **like this**, are explained in the Glossary.

# Contents

# About mysteries

For centuries, people have been puzzled and fascinated by mysterious places, creatures and events. Is there really a monster in Loch Ness? Did the lost city of Atlantis ever really exist? Are crop circles messages from aliens, or simply clever hoaxes? Is there life on Mars or Venus? Do strange creatures like vampires and werewolves come out at night?

Some of these mysteries have baffled scientists, who have spent years trying to find the answers. But just how far can science go? Can it really explain the unexplained? Are there some mysteries which science simply cannot solve? Read on, and try to make up your own mind ...

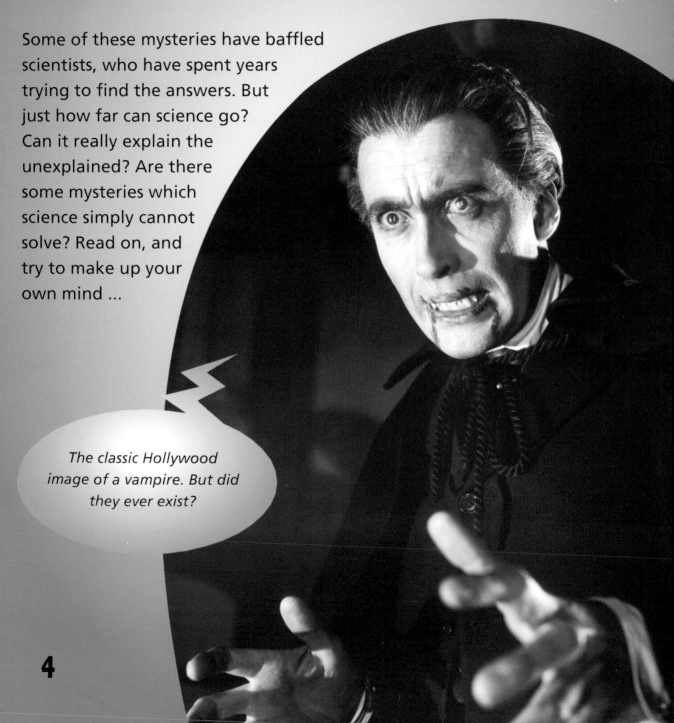

*The classic Hollywood image of a vampire. But did they ever exist?*

This book tells you about vampires and werewolves. It looks at where the stories about vampires and werewolves come from, what people thought they looked like, some eyewitness accounts and real-life stories of vampires and werewolves, and some theories about what they could really be.

## What are vampires?

When you hear the word 'vampire', what do you think of? It's probably a terrifying, **undead** human figure who goes out at night to find victims and drink their blood. This is what people have believed for hundreds of years. You probably also imagine the figure wearing a long black cape, having two long, sharp fangs, sleeping in a coffin during the day and turning into a bat at night. Most of these ideas come from novels, films and television shows.

## What are werewolves?

When you hear the word 'werewolf', what do you think of? A person who changes into a vicious wolf, kills and eats people, and then turns back into a human? This is what a **mythical** werewolf is supposed to do. You may have other ideas about werewolves, perhaps that a werewolf looks like a person with a hairy face and hands, has pointy ears, and a mouth full of grubby teeth, but you have probably got these ideas from the movies or television!

Most serious scientists would say that vampires and werewolves are just **myths**. But is there anything science can do to prove whether vampires and werewolves really exist? Prepare your self for some grisly stuff!

# Beginnings of a mystery

It's impossible to tell when and where the first stories about vampires and werewolves were told, but these tales have been around for hundreds, if not thousands, of years. They were originally told in times when most people were religious and very **superstitious**, too. There were no communications like television and telephones, which meant that people only heard about news and events by word of mouth. Many stories of strange creatures passed around.

## Home of the vampires

There are stories of hideous creatures that sucked blood from their victims from all over the world. They come from China, from North and South America, and from Africa. But the most famous stories come from countries in Eastern Europe, such as Hungary, Albania, Romania and Greece.

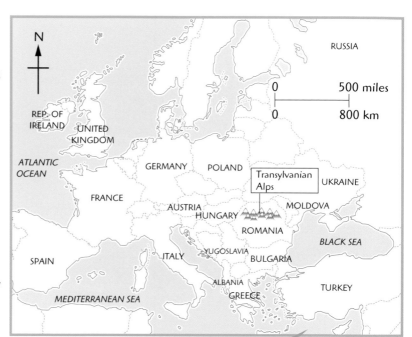

In the **Middle Ages**, the people of Eastern Europe really believed in vampires. Members of the Christian church argued about what vampires were and where they came from. If people thought that there was a vampire about, they dug up graves, searching for people whose bodies had not rotted away.

Many vampire stories come from a region of modern-day Romania called Transylvania.

The huge modern-day interest in vampires has come from novels and films made in the last 150 years. This is when the caped, fanged figure we all know appeared. The novel that really started it all was *Dracula*, which was published in 1897.

## Ancient werewolves

Some ancient Greek **physicians** believed that certain people could transform themselves into various animal forms. The ancient Greeks and Romans believed that their gods could take many different forms, too. And in Greek mythology, the king Lycaon was turned into a wolf by Zeus. Even in ancient times, Europe was famous for werewolves. Nearly 2500 years ago, the Greek historian Herodotus wrote about people in central Europe who turned into wolves.

In the Middle Ages, real wolves were much more common than they are today. They killed many people in rural villages. But the villagers often blamed other people for these deaths, claiming that the murderers had turned into wolves to do the deeds.

A woodcut of a werewolf attack from the 16th century.

# Vampire myths

Before investigating whether science can help to explain what vampires and werewolves are, we need to know exactly what the **myths** about them say. What are they supposed to look like, and how are they supposed to act?

## The vampire lifestyle

If vampires really exist, what are they? For a start, a vampire is a **supernatural** creature, so it does not obey the natural laws of physics, chemistry or biology. In the myths, a vampire is a spirit or soul that lives in a dead body. In the day, it sleeps in the grave or coffin where the dead person was buried.

A vampire can only survive by drinking human blood. This gives it life energy or 'life force'. So at night, the vampire leaves its coffin or grave and finds victims to attack. The human victims cannot defend themselves, because vampires have supernatural strength. A vampire's victim becomes weak and dies from loss of blood, and then becomes a vampire, too.

## Not a pretty face

Myths about vampires say that even in human form, a vampire has features that make it recognizable. Vampires from Eastern Europe, and especially from Transylvania (see map on page 6), have very skinny bodies and pale skin. They are said to have eyebrows that meet in the middle, bright, clear eyes that **hypnotize** their victims, pointed **canine** teeth that they use to pierce skin, very red lips, and very nasty breath! They also have long, sharp fingernails and hair on the palms of their hands.

Vampires from other parts of the world have slightly different features. For example, vampires from Mexico are said to have no flesh on their skulls, and vampires from Russia are said to have purple faces.

According to myths, vampires can also change shape to take the form of other animals. Most famously, they can change into bats, but they can also change into wolves. Worse still, they can control other night creatures and force them to help with their evil deeds.

*This woodcut shows Vlad the Impaler, an historic vampire from Eastern Europe.*

# Werewolf myths

Here you can find out what **mythical** werewolves are supposed to look like and what nasty deeds they are supposed to do. Vampires and werewolves have some common features. Like vampires, werewolves are **supernatural** creatures. In fact, in **medieval** times people thought that if a werewolf died, it became a vampire.

A werewolf is a living person who has the ability to change magically into a wolf, normally just for a few hours, but sometimes permanently. When it is in wolf form, a werewolf hunts human victims, tears out their throats and eats them! Like vampires, werewolves have supernatural strength when they are in wolf form, so their human victims have no hope of escape.

People of Eschenbach, Germany hunting a werewolf that terrorized their town in the 17th century.

# Hairy hands

Mythical werewolves are harmless when they are in human form. Some do not even know that they become werewolves. But they are supposed to have strange features, often similar to those of vampires. Like vampires, they have pale skin. Hairiness is another common feature! Werewolves' eyebrows meet in the middle, and their hands and feet are more hairy than normal people's. They also have long, pointy fingernails that are red, like the colour of blood, and small, pointy ears.

When in wolf form, most mythical werewolves look like real wolves and walk on all fours. The only difference is that they are slightly bigger than real wolves. Some werewolves are said to stand on two legs and retain some of their human features, a bit like the werewolves you see in films. Whatever they look like, they are fierce, strong, fast and, most importantly, very cunning. However, werewolves in wolf form can still speak and their eyes look like human eyes.

*Do you think this bear could be a shape changing person?*

## Shape changing

*Werewolves are an example of a mythical creature that can change shape from one animal to another. This ability is called shape-changing, shape-shifting or morphing. There are many other examples of shape-changing supernatural creatures around the world, such as man-tigers and bears in Asia and man-lizards in New Zealand.*

# Vampire stories

Although there are many stories about vampires killing people in local communities, there are no reliable eyewitness accounts, either from people who say they have been attacked, or by people who say they have seen an attack in progress. However, there are reports of deaths that appear to have been caused by vampires. Worse still, there are some rather nasty cases of real people killing victims in the way that vampires would. These cases must have fuelled the vampire **myth**.

## Poland, 19th century

In 1870, in the Polish town of Kantrzyno, a man called Franz von Poblocki died of an illness called consumption. He was buried in the local churchyard. Two weeks later his son Anton died of the same illness, and other members of the family fell ill, too. The family believed that Franz must have become a vampire! They decided to stop him before he took any more of their 'life blood'. With the help of a vampire expert called Dzigielski they sneaked into the churchyard at night, dug up Franz's body and cut off its head. They were discovered doing the deed and put on trial. In court they claimed that they had acted in self-defence. The judge agreed and let them off.

*Digging up the dead, believing their father was a vampire saw the Poblocki family put on trial.*

## France, 15th century

This is a story of a real person who behaved like a vampire. Gilles de Rais was a French aristocrat who lived in the 15th century. He was a soldier who fought against the English with the famous female military leader, Joan of Arc. Gilles de Rais was found guilty of murdering 150 people to get their blood and drink it, helped by his servants. He was executed, in a very horrible way, in 1440.

## Hungary, 17th century

Elizabeth de Bathory was another real person who behaved like a vampire. She was a Polish countess who lived in 17th-century Hungary. Elizabeth liked to bath in human blood, because she believed that it would keep her young. She killed several hundred people to get blood for her bath, but was caught when the authorities broke into her castle. In 1611, she was imprisoned for life – she would have been executed if she had not been a countess.

*The 17th-century Countess Elizabeth de Bathory. Was she a vampire?*

# Werewolf stories

Here are some eyewitness accounts from people who claimed to have seen werewolves. Just as there are cases of real people who acted like vampires, there are cases of people who acted like werewolves, but they were not able to turn into wolves like the werewolves in stories.

## Germany, 18th century

This event is said to have happened near the German town of Caasberg in 1721. A farmer and his wife were cutting hay in a field with other farm workers. Suddenly the wife said that she could not carry on working and left the field. She told her husband to look out for wild animals and that if an animal came near, he should throw his hat at it and run away. A few minutes later, a wolf was seen coming towards the field. As instructed, the farmer threw his hat, which distracted the wolf while another man ran behind it and stabbed it with a fork. Instantly, the wolf changed back into human form. To their horror, it was the farmer's wife!

## France, 18th century

In 1764, a series of nasty murders and animal killings started in southern France. The murders went on for three years, during which time 40 people were killed and more than 100 others were injured. Survivors said that they had been attacked by a huge red creature, with scales and a big mouth full of sharp teeth, that could run like the wind. It was known as the Beast of Gevaudan. In 1767, a huge wolf was trapped and killed. The attacks suddenly stopped, but there were still rumours that a werewolf had been responsible.

The 18th-century wolf known as the Beast of Gevaudan.

## France, 16th century

Frenchman Jaques Rollet confessed in court that he had used a magic **ointment** to change himself into a wolf. But he said that he only acted like a wolf. He still looked like a person except for hairy, wolf-like hands and feet.

## Germany, 16th century

Peter Stubbe was an infamous murderer who killed hundreds of people. He was eventually captured, and convicted of being a werewolf. It is said that he turned himself into a wolf by putting on a belt made of wolf skin. Stubbe was executed in 1589.

# Vampire theories

There are several theories about what makes a vampire, how to stop people becoming vampires, and how to kill vampires.

## How a vampire is made

In the **myths**, there were many ideas about how people were turned into vampires. The most common was that a vampire was the soul of a dead person. The person had died and been buried, but his or her soul had refused to pass into heaven, hell, or the spirit world. Instead, it had stayed in this world and used the body of the dead person to do its evil deeds.

There were many **superstitions** about why a person's soul might stay in this world. They included that a person was wicked or was condemned by the church, and so could not go to heaven; that he or she was not buried in a proper Christian way; that he or she committed suicide; that he or she died a violent death, such as being murdered; and that he or she was a witch or a werewolf. Some people thought that a vampire was the devil's worker in human form, or a person's body taken over by a spirit to do evil. Any victim of a vampire also became a vampire.

## Projections from the mind

*A different **supernatural** theory is that a vampire is something called an **astral projection**. An astral projection is said to be a physical object that is projected from a person's mind while the person is asleep. Evil spirits or the cruel side of the person's nature take over the projection and make it do evil deeds.*

## Stopping a vampire

There were also theories about how to stop people becoming vampires when they died. These included burying special items, such as cloves of garlic, lemon or bread blessed by a priest, along with the body. These methods were supposed to stop the vampire returning to the body after a night out! Nailing the body into the coffin was also said to work.

Killing vampires required different methods. Hammering a wooden stake, sword or dagger through a vampire's heart while it slept was said to turn the body to dust. Exposing the vampire to sunlight was also said to work.

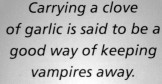

*Carrying a clove of garlic is said to be a good way of keeping vampires away.*

# Werewolf theories

There are several theories about what makes a werewolf and how to kill werewolves.

## How a werewolf is made

Different parts of the world have different theories about how an ordinary person can become a werewolf. They include sleeping outdoors when there is a full moon, being born when there is a full moon, drinking water from a stream that a wolf has drunk from and drinking from a footprint made by a real wolf.

According to **superstition**, there are several ways that a werewolf can turn from human form into wolf form and back again. These include wearing a skin from a real wolf, wearing a girdle of animal skin and rubbing magic **ointment** on the body. As soon as the skin or ointment is removed, the werewolf returns to human form. Some werewolves can control when they turn from human form into wolf form, but others cannot.

*Wearing the skin of a real wolf was said to turn a werewolf into wolf form.*

In **medieval** times, one theory was that werewolves had skin with hair on the inside. To turn from human to wolf, they simply turned their skin inside out! Many suspected werewolves were killed when angry mobs cut them open to try to find their inward-pointing fur.

## Identifying a werewolf

According to **myths**, a werewolf can be turned back to human form by saying its human name, by hitting it three times on the forehead, or by making a sign of the cross. Another **supernatural** theory is called 'wound-doubling'. This means that if a werewolf is injured while it is in wolf form, the wound will still be there when the werewolf turns back to human form. People who claimed to have injured a werewolf would look for a person with the same wound.

*The occultist Eliphas Levi.*

## Astral projections

*Some people believe in another supernatural theory, that a werewolf who attacks people is a projection from the mind of a sleeping person. A 19th-century **occultist**, called Eliphas Levi, said that a person's 'sidereal body' could go out into the countryside at night, while their physical body was asleep, dreaming about being a wolf.*

# Vampire science

There is one theory about vampires that is scientific. Some doctors now think that people who were thought to be vampires in fact had terrible diseases. This theory does not explain how **mythical** vampires could exist, but it does explain where some vampire stories might have come from.

## Mixed up genes

Genes are the complex chemicals in each cell of your body that control how your body grows and the job that each cell does. They are passed on from generation to generation. Sometimes people are born with small faults in their genes, which are called genetic mutations.

One rare disease caused by genetic mutations is Erythropoietic Protoporphyria. This disease was common in noble families of Eastern Europe in the **Middle Ages**. It makes the skin, eyes and teeth look red, and also makes the upper lip pull back, revealing the teeth. If sufferers go out in sunshine, their lips and skin crack and bleed.

Erythropoietic Protoporphyria was not identified as a proper disease until the 19th century, so doctors in the Middle Ages did not know how to treat it. They locked the poor sufferer in a dark place during day to reduce the bleeding, and only let them out at night. The sufferer was also made to drink blood to replace what they lost through bleeding. Unfortunately, the disease was normally fatal.

*The forests of Transylvania, where the disease Erythropoietic Protoporphyria was common.*

You can imagine the rumours that spread about strange-looking children with red eyes, and their top teeth showing, who drank blood, and only came out of their castles at night!

## Did vampires have rabies?

*Rabies is a disease caused by a* **virus**. *It is spread when an infected animal bites another animal. Among the animals that can get rabies are dogs, bats and humans. Rabies makes people so aggressive that they sometimes try to bite and it stops them sleeping, so that they are awake at night. Rabies also makes people sensitive to things such as bright lights and smells, and causes face muscles to contract at random, making the lips curl back in a snarl. Perhaps people with rabies were mistaken for vampires in the past. There is evidence of a serious rabies outbreak in Hungary in the 1720s, when many vampire stories began.*

# Animal vampires

Drinking blood may be a horrible way to live, but its not as strange as it seems. The only real vampires that we know exist today are not humans, but animals. There are several animals that feed on the blood of other animals. These include insects, leeches and the famous vampire bat, which may have led to stories about vampires turning into bat form at night.

## Vampire bats

The vampire bat lives in Central and South America. Like other bats, it is a **mammal**, but it is the only mammal that lives on blood. The vampire bat is quite small, not much bigger than a mouse. It searches for sleeping animals to drink blood from using **echolocation** (bouncing sounds) to help it. Its victims include large animals, such as cows and sheep.

Because of its name and its two long sharp teeth, people often think that the vampire bat has two fangs, like a **mythical** vampire, and that it uses them to suck blood out. In fact, the vampire bat does not suck blood and does not kill.

*Here you can see the sharp teeth of a vampire bat.*

It actually has very sharp front teeth that it uses to cut a tiny piece of skin from its victim. Then for a few minutes it drinks the blood that oozes slowly from the wound. The blood does not clot, because the bat's saliva contains a chemical that stops clotting. The sleeping victim often never knows that the bat has taken its blood. Vampire bats sometimes drink so much blood from their victims that they cannot take off until the meal is digested!

## Insect blood-suckers

Many species of insects live on the blood of mammals and birds. They are called **parasitic** insects. They include fleas, mosquitoes and midges. These insects feed by sticking their sharp mouthparts into the skin of their victim to find small blood vessels near the surface, called capillaries. Then they suck out the blood through a narrow tube.

*A mosquito taking a meal from a human.*

# Werewolf science

At the moment, science cannot explain how humans could turn into wolves. But there is one scientific theory about werewolves that may explain where the **myths** about them came from. As with vampires, the theory is a medical one.

## Lycanthropy

The word 'lycanthrope' comes from the Greek words *lycos*, which means 'wolf', and *anthropos*, which means 'man'. So lycanthrope literally means 'wolf-man'. In ancient Greece, the word meant somebody who had been transformed into a beast.

Today, the words 'werewolf' and 'lycanthrope' are sometimes used to mean the same thing, but they don't. A lycanthrope is a person who only imagines that they have been transformed into a wolf. A **mythical** werewolf is someone who actually transforms into a wolf by some magical or **supernatural** power.

A lycanthrope suffers from a mental illness called lycanthropy. A person suffering from lycanthropy imagines that he or she looks and behaves like a wolf, but in reality the sufferer has not changed in appearance in any way. Lycanthropes often say that they have their wolf fur on the inside of their skin, which is why they look like a human. **Psychiatrists** call lycanthropy a form of delusion. The illness was first seen in the 7th century, when sufferers were described as moving on four legs and howling at night!

# Brain poisoning

Another theory about werewolf stories comes from **medieval** times. Poor people often suffered from dream-like **hallucinations** that are thought to have been caused by eating damp grain. The damp grain often had a type of **fungus**, called claviceps, growing on it. It is known as **ergotized** grain. This fungus makes a chemical, called lysergic acid diethylamide. We now know that if it is taken in large doses, this chemical can cause people to think they are turning into an animal! How many peasants thought they were turning into wolves because of eating damp grain? Similar hallucinations were brought on by eating bits of plants and animals given to people by magicians and sorcerers.

*Ergotized grain can cause hallucinations. Can this explain beliefs about werewolves?*

# Stories and films

The **mythical** stories of vampires and werewolves are both fascinating and scary. It's no wonder that many novels, including children's stories, have been written about them, and dozens of films and popular television programmes (including comedies!) have been made about them.

## Dracula

The first vampire and werewolf novels were written in the 19th century, when horror stories became popular. One of the first was *Varney the Vampire or the Feast of Blood*, published in 1847. But most famous of all was the novel that became the inspiration for many films – *Dracula*. *Dracula* was written by the Irish novelist, Bram Stoker, and published in 1897.

In the novel, the vampire Dracula travels to England to find victims. He is hunted down by the fiancé of one of the women he attacks, along with a vampire expert. They eventually follow Dracula to his castle in Transylvania and kill him.

*This portrait of Count Dracula comes from a castle in Austria.*

The vampire in the story, Count Dracula, was based on a real person, who lived in the 15th century. His name was Vlad Tepes. He became Prince Vlad IV of Wallachia, an area in modern-day Romania. Vlad was not a nice person to know. He was a **tyrant** in his own country, and apparently killed about 40,000 enemy prisoners of war by impaling them on sharp sticks. This was how he earned one of his nicknames – Vlad the Impaler (see page 9). His other nickname was Romanian for 'son of the devil' or 'son of the dragon' – Draculaea. Dracula's castle was probably modelled on the Csejthe, the castle of Elizabeth de Bathory (see page 13).

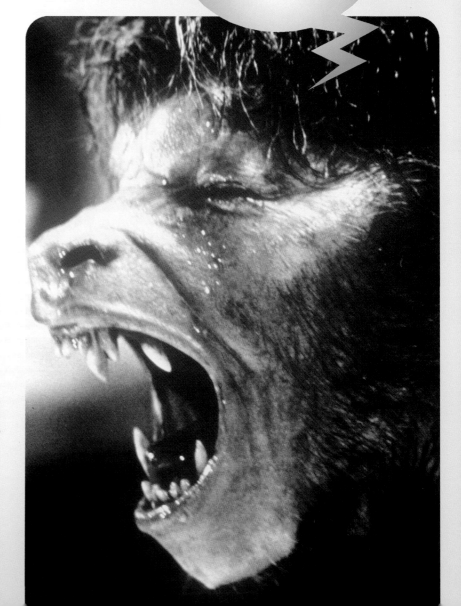

*People are still fascinated by shape-changing creatures. This is from the film* American Werewolf in London.

## Werewolf tales

There have also been novels and films about werewolves. One of the earliest stories was *William and the Werewolf*, written in France in the late 12th century. Films include Hammer Horror's *Curse of the Werewolf* (1960). Stories about other shape-changing creatures are also popular, especially in superhero comic stories.

# In conclusion

Can science really solve the mystery of vampires and werewolves? What's certain is that, at the moment, science cannot explain **mythical** vampires or werewolves. It cannot explain how a spirit could take over a body, as a vampire does. Neither can it explain how a human could transform into a wolf as a werewolf does, or any other form of shape-changing.

Scientists tend to dismiss eyewitness accounts of vampires and werewolves, because they mostly come from so long ago, when people were very **superstitious**, and knew little about science and medicine. The scientists' argument is made stronger because there are hardly any cases of people seeing vampires or werewolves for real. There is just no reliable evidence for them. On the other hand, some eyewitness accounts can be explained by the medical theories.

But there is no doubt that some people in the past have been convinced that vampires and werewolves existed, and that they were very scared of them. Some people still do believe it.

*The logo of the modern Dracula Society.*

CREDO QUIA IMPOSSIBLE

# What do you think?

Now that you have read about vampires and werewolves and the possible explanations for them, can you draw any conclusions? Do you feel that you can dismiss any of the theories without investigating them further, even though some have no evidence to support them? Do you believe that **supernatural** creatures like the mythical vampires and werewolves could exist? Or do you only believe things that science has proved? Do you have any theories of your own?

Can we accept evidence of vampires and werewolves from hundreds of years ago, that may have been passed on by word of mouth before being written down? Do you think the **myths** continue because they are fascinating and scary? Will you keep an eye out for people with red eyes, pointy fingernails and hairy hands?!

*A perfect night for vampires and werewolves!*

Try to keep an open mind. Bear in mind that if scientists throughout history had not bothered to investigate things that appeared to be strange or mysterious, many scientific discoveries may never have been made.

# Glossary

**astral projection** physical object or being that is projected in some way from a person's mind. There is no scientific evidence that astral projections exist.

**canine** describes anything to do with the dog family (including wolves). Canine teeth are the extra-long, pointed teeth on either side of a dog's jaw.

**echolocation** way of finding the position of an object by sending out sounds and listening for any echoes that bounce off objects. Bats use echolocation to find their way and to hunt for food.

**ergotized** describes grain that has a particular type of fungus growing on it

**fungus** organism that is not an animal or plant and that lives on decaying plants or animals. Mushrooms, toadstools and moulds are all fungi.

**hallucination** something that you think you hear or see, but that does not really exist

**hypnotize** put a person into a state like sleep, but in which they obey commands and answer questions

**mammal** animal that is warm-blooded, has a backbone and feeds its young on milk

**medieval** describes anything from the Middle Ages or that happened in the Middle Ages

**Middle Ages** the name given to the period in European history from about AD 1000 to about AD 1450

**myth** traditional story or a common idea or belief that is false

**mythical** describes something, such as a werewolf, that appears in myths

**occultist** person who believes in and studies supernatural events

**ointment** cream that is rubbed onto the skin

**parasitic** describes an organism that lives and feeds on another organism

**physician** doctor or healer

**psychiatrist** doctor who studies and treats mental diseases

**supernatural** creature or event that cannot be explained by the science that we understand today

**superstition** belief in something supernatural

**superstitious** describes a person who believes in superstitions

**tyrant** someone who is an oppressive or cruel ruler

**undead** describes a supernatural being that lives in the body of a dead person

**virus** micro-organism that brings disease, only visible through a microscope

# Index